Weekly Reader Books presents

Donald and the Fish that Walked

By Edward R. Ricciuti
Pictures by Syd Hoff

A Science I CAN READ Book

Harper & Row, Publishers
New York, Evanston, San Francisco, London

DONALD AND THE FISH THAT WALKED
Text copyright © 1974 by Edward Raphael Ricciuti
Illustrations copyright © 1974 by Syd Hoff
All rights reserved. No part of this book may be used or reproduced in any manner
whatsoever without written permission except in the case of brief quotations em-
bodied in critical articles and reviews. Printed in the United States of America.
For information address Harper & Row, Publishers, Inc., 10 East 53rd Street, New
York, N.Y. 10022. Published simultaneously in Canada by Fitzhenry & Whiteside
Limited, Toronto.
Library of Congress Catalog Card Number: 74-2609
Trade Standard Book Number: 06-024997-8
Harpercrest Standard Book Number: 06-024998-6

For Donna, Mac,
and the little Buckleys

Donald's dog was barking

outside the house.

"If Sam is barking at

that cat again,"

thought Donald,

"we are both in trouble."

He ran out to Sam.

Sam was not barking at a cat.

He was barking at a fish.

It was walking.

It was walking

across the lawn.

"Yow!" said Donald.

The fish was pink.

It had bright eyes.

They were like

hard, shiny stones.

"Watch out, Sam!" said Donald.

"That fish might be dangerous."

But the fish just kept walking.

It walked to a ditch

and plopped into the water.

"Creepy," said Donald.

At dinner, Donald said,

"I saw a fish in our backyard.

It was walking."

"Now, Donald," said his mother,

"fish do not walk.

They swim in water."

The next morning

Donald met

Lenny and Jonathan.

"I saw a walking fish,"

said Donald.

"Aw," said Jonathan,

"I bet you saw a frog."

"I think it was a siren,"

said Lenny.

"Don't be dumb," said Donald.

"Sirens are in police cars."

"That shows how much

you know," said Lenny.

"Some kinds of salamanders
are called sirens," he said.
"They are long and skinny
like fish."
"Oh," said Donald. "*Those* sirens.

15

"Everybody knows what they are.

But I saw a fish.

And it walked," he said.

Lenny laughed.

"And I saw a flying alligator,"

he said.

Later, Donald went to the ditch.

He put a worm on a fishhook.

Sometimes Donald felt sorry

for worms.

But he had to catch that fish

to show Lenny and Jonathan.

"Hey, I've got something!"

Donald shouted.

He pulled up the pink fish.

But it wiggled off the hook

back into the water.

"Phooey," said Donald.

That evening,

Donald's father said,

"Some strange new fish are living

here in South Florida.

They are catfish

that can walk on land."

23

"That is what I saw," said Donald.

"Poor Donald," said his mother.

"You really did see a walking fish.

And we didn't believe you."

The next day,

Donald, Lenny, and Jonathan

went to the ditch.

They saw Mr. Walter.

He worked at the laboratory

near Donald's house.

A fish flopped around

in Mr. Walter's net.

It was pink.

It had bright, shiny eyes.

"Hey," said Donald,

"a walking catfish."

"Right," said Mr. Walter.

"They are all over the place."

Donald poked Lenny in the ribs.

"Some siren!" Donald said.

"It is no joke," said Mr. Walter.

"Walking catfish are real pests.

We want to get rid of them.

They don't belong around here."

"Don't belong here?" asked Donald.

"Right," said Mr. Walter.

"The real home

of the walking catfish

is far away in Asia."

"How did they get

over here?" asked Jonathan.

"People brought the catfish here

for their fish pools," said Mr. Walter.

"But the catfish got away."

"How?" asked Donald.

"By walking," said Mr. Walter.

"They just walk

from one pond to another."

Mr. Walter added,

"And they breathe air,

so they can stay out of water

for a long time.

They lay lots of eggs, too.

Soon there may be

more walking catfish

than any other kind of fish."

"What's wrong with that?"

asked Donald.

"I caught one. They are fun."

"Before the catfish came,"

said Mr. Walter,

"there was plenty of food

for all the fish

that lived here.

But now, the catfish

are eating all the food.

They are crowding out

the other fish.

"If this keeps up

only the catfish

will be left," he said.

"I guess it is better

to have lots of fish," said Donald.

"Not just one kind."

"You are right," said Mr. Walter.

"The walking catfish

just don't fit in here."

39

Lenny made a face.

"Whoever brought the catfish here,"
he said, "was dumb."

"Well," said Mr. Walter,

"they didn't know
the catfish would get away.
But bad things can happen
when people put animals
where they don't belong.
The catfish might invade
the whole state.

40

"But they don't like cold,"

said Mr. Walter.

"We hope it gets cold enough

to stop them."

42

"I still don't believe

a fish can walk," said Lenny.

Mr. Walter dumped the catfish

on the ground.

The catfish curved its tail.

It pushed against the ground.

Then it pulled itself along

on its two front fins.

"It's a super-fish,"

said Donald.

"It's scary," said Lenny.

That night,

Donald and his father

went out for hamburgers.

Donald ate a big one,

with mustard and a pickle.

On the way home,

Donald's father stopped the car

and looked out the window.

"I can't believe it," he said.

A bunch of catfish

were crossing the road.

They pushed and wiggled

into the grass

on the other side of the road.

49

"It's the catfish invasion!"

yelled Donald.

"They are going to

take over everything."

"Calm down, Donald,"

said his father.

"But they are crowding out

the other fish," said Donald.

"Soon there will be nothing

but walking catfish!" he yelled.

A long time passed.

Donald got used to seeing

walking catfish.

They were everywhere.

Donald was getting tired
of catching walking catfish
when he went fishing.

Then one day

his mother said,

"Put on some blankets tonight."

"Aw, Mom," said Donald,

"it's warm outside."

"The newspaper says

we will have frost tonight,"

said his mother.

"Sometimes it gets cold even

here in South Florida, you know,"

she said.

When night came,

Donald could see his breath

in the air.

The next morning

Donald went outside.

He saw someone

by the ditch.

It was Mr. Walter.

He was scooping up fish

in his net.

The fish were walking catfish,

and they were dead.

"The cold killed

lots of walking catfish,"

said Mr. Walter.

"Too bad it won't stay cold

long enough

to kill them all," he said.

"But now we know

they won't take over."

"Then it's the end

of the catfish invasion,"

said Donald.

"That's right," said Mr. Walter,

"unless the catfish

get used to the cold."

The sun began

to warm the day.

A turtle came out of the water

onto a log.

A bug swam in the water,

and a minnow ate it.

Out of the corner of his eye

Donald saw something else.

A pink fish

with whiskers

and bright eyes

was sliding down

the side of the ditch.

61

Then it disappeared

into the water.

Author's Note

The scientific name of the walking catfish is *Clarias batrachus*. It comes from southeastern Asia, where the climate is warm. For many years people in the United States kept it as an aquarium pet. Some walking catfish at a fish farm in Florida escaped. They spread through southern Florida. Scientists learned about them in March 1967, when a walking catfish was caught by a fisherman. Other walking catfish walked and swam through the many drainage ditches of southern Florida. The catfish had many young. Soon there were so many walking catfish that they upset the balance of nature. However, a cold spell finally killed many of them. The walking catfish is about two feet long. It has a special set of organs that let it breathe air. Its spines are venomous.